A Journey through Grief

Alla Renée Bozarth, Ph.D.

CompCare Publishers
2415 Annapolis Lane
Minneapolis, Minnesota 55441

Bozarth, Alla Renée, 1947-
   A journey through grief / Alla Renée Bozarth.
   p.64 cm.

ISBN 0-89638-204-4
   1. Grief. 2. Bereavement—Psychological aspects.
I. Title.
BF575.G7B685   1990
155.9′37—dc20   90-32987
                                                                      CIP

Cover design by Susan Rinek
Interior design by Lillian Svec

Inquiries, orders, and catalog requests should be addressed to
CompCare Publishers
2415 Annapolis Lane
Minneapolis, Minnesota 55441
Call toll free 800/328-3330
(Minnesota residents 612/559-4800)

6	5	4	3	2	1
95	94	93	92	91	90

Note to the reader: This booklet is a transcription of an original audiotape by Dr. Alla Renée Bozarth, titled "Life Is Goodbye, Life Is Hello." The material is not a duplication of Dr. Bozarth's book by the same name, but some of the poetry selections from the book are repeated here.

Acknowledgments

Author's poems first published in other books

From *Sparrow Songs*, René Bozarth and Alla Bozarth-Campbell, St. Paul's Press and Wisdom House Press, 1982

> "Parting"
> "Dance for Me When I Die"
> "Love Mantra for Letting Go"

From *Life Is Goodbye, Life Is Hello*, Grieving Well through All Kinds of Loss, Alla Renée Bozarth, CompCare Publishers, 1982 and 1986

> "Good-bye Means God Be with You"
> "Scars"
> "Daughter-rite"
> "Continue Becoming the Person You Want to Be"
> "Two Houses"
> "Life after Death"
> "Reincarnation"
> "Journey"
> "Loving the Body"
> "After Dismembering"
> "Awakening"

Journey

One way or another
more naked when we die
than at birth.
Emptied.

Unharnessed.
Unencumbered.
Untangled.
Allowed

for the journey
only as much
as will fit
into the hand
of God.

A Journey through Grief

I speak to you today, my friend, as a companion on a journey. I speak from my own experience as one who has gone on a grief journey several times. I speak to you on the basis of what I have learned personally, in my soul, about letting go.

I bear down hard
on all life's losses.
Each one is unique, it's true.
As no love is the same,
no loss is.

I have to let each one
out of me separately,
give each loss the scream
that belongs to its
own love's ecstacy.

If I succeed, one by one,
in letting go, in remembering
myself, I may again know
that dreamy sweetness,
the smells of love,
what life is, the feeling
of emergence from bliss.

To surrender to one's own grief and to become actively engaged in it require tremendous courage. This courage is vastly different from putting up a good front, showing a cheerful face to our friends when we're really hurting.

Real courage is...owning up to the fact that we face a terrifying task...admitting that we are appropriately frightened...identifying sources of strength and help, both outside and within ourselves...and then going ahead and doing what needs to be done.

Grief is a passion, something that happens to us, something to endure. We can be stricken with it, we can be victims of it, we can be stuck in it. Or, we can meet it, get through it, and become quiet victors through the honest and courageous process of grieving.

And how might I describe the process and its many feelings or absence of feeling?

I feel empty!
  I feel frozen.
    I feel small, smaller and smaller!
      I feel buried alive, put to sleep.
I feel dead.
I feel numb.
I feel nothing.

Slowly, as the natural anesthesia of the heart wears off, my metaphors may change.

I feel myself underwater,
  unable to move or breathe or see light.
I feel myself in a place with no top
  or bottom,
  a place with no walls and no protection.
I feel myself trapped in a burning room.
I feel myself shredded.
I feel myself on fire.

And where is the merciful numbness now? Such cataclysmic feelings may occur that it will take constant effort to unravel and feel each one clearly, and I wonder—do I want to bother?

Usually, there is an underlying pattern to these feelings. When feelings first emerge, they may be muddled and overlapping, so that boundaries between them differ, dim, dissolve. This may lead to the panic which an earlier stage of shock might have prevented, feelings like...

a sense of getting nowhere...
of flying faster and faster...
of spinning in tight circles.

A person might begin by feeling some clear sense of relief, perhaps that the long ordeal leading to this final loss is now over, and then an almost simultaneous resentment at having been put through the ordeal, followed by guilt—guilt at hundreds of haunting little irrational images of failure or malice—guilt at feeling relieved—guilt at feeling resentful.

Then may come doubt and distrust of one's self or others. Then anger, sadness, rage, despair, and finally the embarrassing, out-of-place giddiness that comes with complete fatigue.

All of these responses may crash in upon one's consciousness with a host of others. It is a little like being mad, glad, sad, and scared—all at once.

Confusion reigns.

The degree of intensity and the particular appearance of any of these feelings depend entirely on the individual and on the special circumstances and the nature of the loss.

Each person has a unique emotional life, and so a unique feeling pattern will emerge in grief, but many of these feelings are common to everyone who experiences loss.

One of the dictionary definitions of *grievous* is "causing physical suffering." Many people overlook or are surprised by the physical side of grief. It is very real and it bears attending. The most common physical symptom of deep grief is low energy. You may need a lot of extra sleep. Be sure to allow for it.

Sleep is more than just escape. Your body needs more rest, just as your soul does, and you may need the necessary dream time of extra sleep. You may tire more quickly than usual and feel generally fatigued and your body may not be as dependable as usual. Or, you may be among the few people who experience a hyperkinetic reaction and have intense bursts of physical energy.

A dear friend of mine was once driven by grief to do the work of three people to burn off her pain through physical exertion. She told me how she scrubbed her kitchen floor in the middle of the night with tears streaming into the wash bucket, working her muscles into exhaustion, before she could finally find rest in a deep sleep.

It is possible to take precautions against illness, such as the use of appropriate vitamins, proper diet, exercise, even if it's only a short walk a day, and, of course, rest. But perhaps the best precaution against the body's suffering of loss is to allow the soul the fullness of the experience. We can help ourselves to wholeness, to well-being, through the absorption of loss, not only by feeling the loss, but by giving ourselves constant positive messages, encouraging our organisms' self-healing functions.

You may notice feeling off balance or dizzy. You may list to one side when you walk. You may notice being uncoordinated, having weaker vision, mis-hearing or mis-seeing, especially when you read. You may experience a temporary loss of hair. Your appetite and sleeping patterns may be erratic, or the opposite of what they normally are.

You may feel drugged without having taken any drugs, or have a feeling of not being in sync with your own body, a looseness or coming apart from the inside, as if your body were a bell and you were the clanger, moving back and forth and around and sometimes even touching yourself from the inside of your skin.

Concentration on intense, internal processes may make it difficult to navigate in the physical world. Your perception of time and distance may be slightly distorted. If that is true, you must take extra precautions when driving and using potentially dangerous tools, including fork and knife. Should any of these symptoms occur, do not be alarmed.

Take care of your body.
It will heal with the rest of you.

See a physician right away for any physical symptom that worries you.

While you are grieving, your emotional life may be unpredictable and unstable. You may feel that there are gaps in your remembered experience. You may totally forget something you said or did, and be incredulous when it's reported back to you. Your creativity may be impaired or it may be heightened. Your imagination and sense perception may be dulled or intensified. You may be irritable, even if this is out of character for you.

You may alternate between depression and euphoria, between wailing rage and passive resignation. You may be calm and steady, but that would be surprising, if not disturbing, unless your temperament is extremely docile. If you've experienced loss and are hurting, it's reasonable that your responses will be unreasonable. If you see yourself as having any of the symptoms I've mentioned, or if you've created your own unique emotional disruption, don't worry.

The symptoms won't last forever.
You will heal!

Learn to be sensitive to the changes you may be going through and be flexible with your new needs and your new patterns. Allow yourself to experiment with new styles of living and working that may be more appropriate for you right now. These changes need not be permanent, but if they are helpful now, use them.

You may feel, "I'm not myself," and, indeed, you are not the self you were before the injury or loss occurred. You may have a sense of having been wounded or violated. You may feel cut off from others. In intense grief, you may feel cut off from yourself or from God. Do not be alarmed if your attitude toward yourself and others is altered drastically. Eventually, it may be altered for the better.

When emotional injury has occurred, it's especially important to watch and listen to the body. Always, it is the whole person who must be healed. For what hurts one part, hurts the whole in some way. After recognizing how grieving feels and identifying what it does to you uniquely, it's time to look at what you can do about it.

How can grieving be a truly healing activity and not merely a destructive passion? Grieving is more than pain. Pain is always a symptom of some injury—an illness or wound. Pain in grief is a symptom of the spiritual wound caused by loss. To tend to the wound is to heal oneself through the creative struggle and final assimilation of the reality of the loss by the whole physical and spiritual person.

Paradoxically, the way past the pain is to go all the way through it.

To treat the symptom of pain by the distractions of frantic busyness, compulsive drinking, overeating, or other dulling, self-destructive behavior, is only a way of prolonging the healing process. We really hurt more when we compulsively try to hurt less. Still, activities that do heal us are certainly worth pursuing and there are ways to work through pain by grieving well rather than through the tail-spinning, destructive hurting of avoidance and denial.

This constructive kind of hurting is what we feel when we lance an infected wound, or pour iodine over a cut, or force ourselves to get up and walk, no matter how stiff we might feel. And, there are ways to bring about healing which are not necessarily painful.

At the very beginning of the grief process, become aware of ways in which you unnecessarily hurt yourself more. For instance, when you hold yourself in, choking back tears, tightening facial and throat muscles, swallowing down surging emotions, or suffocating feelings, it hurts and it doesn't hurt good—it hurts bad. It hurts in the way a physical wound would hurt if, instead of responding to the pain and bleeding, you ignored it or allowed dirt and gravel to get into it and then, even worse, if you actually ground the dirt and gravel down deep into the wound.

You need to treat a spiritual wound resulting from loss as carefully, tenderly, and realistically as you would treat any physical wound. The treatment would, of course, vary as with a physical wound, depending upon its depth and degree, and on your own unique makeup.

Nature gives us two warning signs when we have been injured physically—one knowable only to us and one that is also visible to others. The first sign, of course, is pain. The second one is bleeding, or perhaps internal bleeding, manifested as swelling. We also have pain and the equivalent of bleeding or swelling in our emotional or spiritual beings. Sometimes injury involves no pain, but serious bleeding, as in a clean and serious severence, caused by some forms of amputation. This same thing exists on an emotional or spiritual level. The important thing is to pay attention to the signs, to act wisely and to respond immediately to the reality of the injury.

The worst thing that can happen with any wound is to ignore it so that it becomes infected. Then one is not only in danger from the original wound, but also from one's own defense mechanisms. The body's response to infection is to produce increasing amounts of white blood cells to work as defensive warriors—antibodies, clustering around the offending invasion of germ organisms. As the body is multiplying its own defenses, tremendous amounts of extra energy may be required, depending on the extent of the wound and the intensity of the infection. A fever may result. An unattended fever can cause serious damage, even death.

Again, the same is true emotionally. Treating an emotional wound involves avoiding the neglect that may result in being hurt, even endangered, by your own defenses. Ultimately, the injured organism heals itself.

> Your body has its own healing wisdom within it—and so does your soul, the expressive container of your emotional life.

Two vital external things are essential to the self-healing process—time and cooperation. Time speaks for itself. A line from a popular song says, so truly, "What a friend we have in time."

Cooperation is what you bring to the healing process. First, you locate the injury. Then do the necessary things to treat the injury. The essential treatment after sustaining the injury of a loss is that you express fully what the loss means to you. Not expressing grief can lead to depression, repression, and even unconscious oppression of yourself or others.

So, seek out persons whom you trust, close friends or relatives, or competent professional persons. Talk to them about your loss and its meaning. Talk until you have exhausted talk. Before you wear out the patience of your friends, relatives, or professional helpers, or become boring even to yourself, there is very much that can be said—and the saying of it will help heal the wound.

What you cannot say, write. You might keep a journal. I once began a journal after many years away from the practice. It was a grief journal, and I used it solely for the self-therapy of grieving. The blank paper could reject none of my pain and was never bored by it the way another human being might have been, or the way I, myself, was becoming.

Besides talking, let yourself cry as often as needed. You need not cry in front of others, if this inhibits you. First, let yourself cry in private. Then gradually entrust your tears to another person. Let yourself ask to be held. Let yourself be held, but choose the person you ask wisely.

It is better to cry in someone else's presence than to do so alone. In deep pain or genuine sorrow, that is true *not* because you need an audience, but because you need a witness to your pain, a witness in the religious sense. You need someone to testify to the validity of your feelings, to acknowledge them and to say yes to the good work you are doing in expressing them.

If you feel too uncomfortable to cry much in front of other persons, or if you worry that you will bore them with your tears, then place yourself in the presence of God, however you may conceive of God, and entrust your tears to that presence. You know, there is a beautiful saying, "As God is my witness..."

If this is not possible for you, then imagine a loving human presence, the memory of someone whose love you have experienced, and let that presence stand by you as you weep. Or perhaps, imagine a loving animal presence. Sometimes even a pet can be sustaining comfort when one is distressed and weeping, sometimes even more than any other human being might.

If you are a person who doesn't cry, or if you need to cry but can't for some reason in this particular situation, an outside stimulus for catharsis may be useful. A movie, play, piece of music, or a book may trigger tears unexpectedly. If you begin crying for a character in a movie or a piece of literature, or weeping over a situation in a song or commercial, no matter how inane it may seem to you, let it be. Let yourself yield to the expressive emotion in the moment, recognizing that you have begun to weep for yourself and thus have reached an important stage in self-healing.

Weeping is only a stage—it won't
     last forever.
So, you needn't be afraid to cry.

Crying is what you do when you can't do any-
thing else, before you are able to find other ways
to express your grief. It's better than doing nothing. For then, your body may internalize the tears
and you may become ill, experiencing actual
bodily symptoms. The body creates vivid metaphors. It may substitute other forms of weeping,
releasing inner excesses in liquid form. Catching
cold, developing watering eyes and draining si-
nuses are obvious symbols of a release that needs
to happen emotionally.

My Russian mother used to tell me that the
Russians had a saying, "Tears are the baptism of
the soul." To be baptized means to be cleansed,
to be reborn, and to be welcomed, and tears contain toxins that are actually physically released
and cleansed from our bodies when we cry.

If your loss cuts deep or if it is an old loss that's
been buried alive without ever having been fully

grieved over, it's important that you not be alone when you do specific grief work. Have human resources available for comfort and reassurance, to ground you, to bring you back to reality in this moment.

If you descend far down into your deep or old pain, you will need someone physically present to help bring you back up to reconnect. A skilled therapist or an understanding friend can be a blessed companion on a journey deep into an intensely felt loss.

Facing your loss can be a death-like experience. You must provide sources of new life for yourself. When you come out the other side, you will be as fresh and perhaps as fragile as a newborn infant.

Talking and crying are fundamental means of self-expression. They allow feelings contained in the body as energy to be released as genuine emotion—energy that literally moves out, presses upward, and is uttered or "out-ered" through the body's natural functions of speech and tears.

Though it may strike you as unnecessary, I want to remind you of the most essential bodily function in connection with grieving—breathing. It is the source of all life. Yet, when we are weighed heavily with the burden of strong and painful feelings, breathing is what we first forget to do.

I've seen people doing grief work who will unconsciously hold their breath for a minute or more, or who slow down their breathing to the point of losing color, but are still unaware of what they're doing to themselves—literally cutting off their own life source. I find it necessary to interrupt them in their work with regular reminders, "Keep breathing, keep breathing."

If you are grieving, make "Keep breathing" your mantra. If you don't know how to breathe fully from the diaphragm, find someone who can teach you and practice it with dedication and discipline until it's natural to you. Then, your body will make you conscious of what you're doing when you fail to breathe fully and rhythmically.

"Keep breathing!"

You might breathe with a prayer or an affirmation in mind. For example, as you breathe in, say to yourself, "I am." And as you breathe out, say to yourself, "In God's hands."

"I am..."
"In God's hands."

It's possible even with the pressure of strong feelings just below the surface to allow oneself to untighten, to unclench, to release and relax without being overwhelmed or destroyed by uncontrollable emotions.

The way to protect yourself is first to recognize that the emotions exist. Recognized, they will not be so inclined to haunt or taunt you as when they are denied, and so must create a disturbance to get attention and respect. Often the clamor we sense just below the surface subsides in great measure once we own our painful feelings: "Yes, this is the way I feel."

"Yes, this is the way I feel."

This makes it possible to begin dealing with the feelings, bit by bit. Have faith in yourself. Your body has the wisdom to call your attention to important aspects of your life that you may be ignoring, and your soul has the same wisdom. Paying attention to this wisdom is the beginning of healing.

While you are grieving, you are in the process of restoring your basic capacity for life. You won't experience great joys or intense pleasures, but for the time being, you can learn to substitute simply satisfying comforts for these.

Develop a new appreciation for the simple sustaining gifts of life—for walking, breathing, sleeping, for nourishing food, especially for kind friends, and for the kindness of strangers. Mere physical well-being can take on new meaning and value for you. Relying on the constancy of your own human life processes can be a working substitute for the joys of life from which you are temporarily cut off.

Value the grieving work you are doing. It's important. Finally, and most importantly here, discover what helps you. No one else can do that for you.

Pace yourself lovingly and remember— this pain won't last forever.

Be sensitive to your own timing. Don't push yourself ahead of your process and don't let others push you because they are uncomfortable with your grief. Let it take as long as it takes, but don't hold on, either. Let the pain go when the time comes. Doing grief work is like being a trapeze artist. Balance and timing are everything. Letting go too soon and holding on too long are equally dangerous. Learn to tolerate the tedium and clumsiness of the process, and trust time. Time is on your side. Continue becoming the person you want to be.

Continue Becoming the Person You Want to Be

The future is like death—
Unknown—
and requires as much faith.
So Becoming
is like Dying.

The lapse between
a single
inbreath/outbreath
a slash or question
mark in time,
the act of transformation

the monarch butterfly knows.
It flies alone.
Sometimes the dead do not know they
have died.
Sometimes the winged one dreams itself
a cocoon.
Everlasting Change comes, all the same.

I've said that time is on your side, but time itself doesn't heal. It only gives us room to free and heal ourselves. Time offers us the eternal present of possibility. We determine that possibility through our decisions and actions. We decide to use the time well. If we waste the gift of time and fail to incorporate past and future into the present moment, which alone is ours, old wounds may not close. A hurtful word may be as painfully present in memory as it was when originally inflicted perhaps ten or even forty years ago.

Most of us are living through grief or grieving through life much of the time, for life is conditioned by small and significant daily losses. On the other side of grief, we can discover the joy and gratitude that come with new and renewed zest—for every loss creates a space and in that space, something new and wonderful may happen.

Our natural state of well-being involves both the grieving and the enjoying inherent in any moment of loss, with its change and chance for renewal. And our habitual greed for more of what we lose is healed, moment by moment, by the practice of gratitude for the gifts of every day, of every moment, and of all our relationships.

Everyone who lives suffers, as well as enjoys—that is true. But not everyone learns to live more fully because of it. Suffering itself has no value. It is the use that one makes of suffering, as it is with all other kinds of experience. Through attitude and action—therein lies the value.

Although suffering teaches nothing, I can decide to teach myself through suffering. I can teach myself to become more human and more loving, more honest and more powerful.

Living through desperation and despair with courage and honesty, we can prepare ourselves to be more understanding of and compassionate toward ourselves and one another—more discerning of the difference between avoidable and un-avoidable suffering—and more determined to eradicate the former from our lives.

Above all, through loss experiences, we can teach ourselves a new kind of joy. This may seem strange, but it's true. We may find a joy which is large enough to contain our pain and to transform it into a new kind of power—the power to make us whole.

Through the power of love, sorrow can deepen the soul and its capacity for joy—and the two can strangely co-exist.

Neither sorrow nor joy negates the other, but both together increase our experience of life and wonder. If you could keep your heart in wonder, you would know that love is the unfolding miracle that expands our joy to include our pain.

If You Could Keep Your Heart in Wonder

> Our love is
> the unfolding
> miracle
>
> that expands
> our joy
> to include
> our pain.

Being able to face fully the reality of loss depends on the balance between personal integrity and creativity. Integrity looks at something and says, "What is, is." Creativity looks at something and asks, "What new thing can come from this?" Integrity forces us to see things as they are. Creativity allows us to use *what is* for the raw material of *what can be.*

People who survive loss and come out of it with restored vigor do so because they are able to meet reality with a certain determination and a certain imagination. They create new skills for themselves to meet a new challenge. They grow themselves into new life. This doesn't sound easy, and it isn't, but *it is possible*. And when it does happen, it's wonderful.

Besides integrity and creativity, trust in yourself is essential in the art of grieving well, just as it is in the art of living well.

Trust yourself...trust your feelings...own your feelings...recognize them as your own.

Feel your feelings. They won't destroy you, because you can learn to express them safely and constructively with the reassuring help of others.

Care for yourself. In coping with grievous loss, make life as healing as possible for yourself. Surround yourself with comforting basics—food, bed, the security of an income, friends, or family. If it's not easy to do this, get the help that you need. If your own biological family is not supportive of you, you can adopt persons whom you trust to be a family for you, to give you the nourishing support you need, with the shared understanding that in time, this support will be mutual, even if it can't be for now.

Provide a nourishing environment for yourself.

Avoid major changes that will uproot you emotionally from the safety and care of loved ones or from a familiar place.

Put major decisions on hold, if you can.

Rely on the security of the familiar until you're more healed. If the familiar is not nourishing, protective, or safe, make external changes which are somehow guaranteed by friendly presences.

Allow yourself to suffer your own healing process, to suffer your own meaning. You need to discover what the loss means to you, and what the healing means as well.

Let it take as long as it takes.

The greater the loss, the longer your recovery may be. The more meaning whatever is lost had for you—or the more of yourself and your life or time you had invested in it—the more of yourself and the more life and time will go into the healing.

There was a flowering crabtree in my backyard some years ago. One autumn the small, hard, red fruit failed to fall off the tree, as it and the leaves died. The light leaves fell according to plan, but the heavier fruit remained, dried up and useless, yet stubbornly clinging to the branches through fall and into winter.

I looked at the tree in February, the fruit still visible under the heavy snow of Minnesota. I thought, "For all your tenacity, spring will come in a few months and you, last season's crab apples, you will have no choice. You will get pushed off those branches by the new shoots coming up from underneath."

In April, I watched that tenacious crab fruit get pushed off the tree by the irrepressible new shoots. Ultimately, life takes the place of death. Dead things get pushed away to make room for more life, or maybe they simply become more life in a way that we don't understand.

Nothing is lost.
Everything *is* always, and is near.

So, the tree taught me something. I'm like that too. No matter how stubbornly I cling to my pain, refusing to let go of my actual loss, to give up my grief, sooner or later if I'm to go on living at all, I will have to give it up. The life inside me will push it all away in its own natural and right time.

Eventually the life inside me will prove to be more stubborn than the death.

In grieving, we embark on a journey through our own soul's seasons...

fall...
   winter...
      then, spring...
         finally, summer once more...

...a journey through death and loss into renewal and life.

Through grieving, we learn new value for the gift of life. We're forced to take less for granted, to be more generous in communicating our gratitude for the life and love that surround us. More generous and spontaneous with praise words.

Life is too short to withhold soul-nourishing compliments...to let deep love go unexpressed... to let people pass through our lives without telling them how much they mean to us.

We need to let ourselves feel and express our growing gratitude for family, for friends, for health, for the healing resources within us.

In grieving, I need to say what was left unsaid and to let myself hear what was left unheard— anger, uncertainty, forgiveness, care, love.

I know that with help I can complete what was left incomplete within myself. I know that I can find my own time and create my own way. I can learn to live creatively with a bruised or broken heart.

A broken heart is a heart made larger and more open than before. And you too can do what you need to do to be healed.

I wish for you the courage to continue and to discover a new possibility for life and for love.

I wish you well and I send you light, until you can see again the light within you.

I invite you now to an interior journey—a healing meditation.

Breathe gently, naturally, with gratitude. Breathe...relax your body...rest...and as you do this, become aware that inside you there is a healing spirit, the resilient radiance of your birthright.

Breathe yourself into the image of a safe and restful place. Take yourself to your own power spot, your place of healing in your imagination. Go there now and open yourself to the inner self-healer. This inner healer is awake now, and ready to assist you with love.

Notice where you are. Find the beauty and the protection around you, and rest in this place in the presence of the healer who is with you. Find an image or a color or a sensation by which you can return to this place of healing whenever you wish.

Continue to rest here and let your mind receive the images of beauty and strength, as I read Psalm 139 to you now:

"Holy One, you have searched me out and known me. You know my sitting down and my rising up. You discern my thoughts from afar. You trace my journeys and my resting places and are acquainted with all my ways. Indeed, there is not a word on my lips but you know it altogether. You press upon me, behind and before. You lay your hand upon me.

"Such knowledge is too wonderful for me. It is so high that I cannot attain to it. Where can I go then from your spirit? Where can I flee from your presence? If I climb up to heaven, you are there. If I make the grave my bed, you are there also. If I take the wings of the morning and dwell in the uttermost parts of the sea, even there your hand will lead me and your right hand hold me fast. If I say, 'Surely the darkness will cover me and the light around me turn to night,' oh, darkness is not dark to you. The night is as bright as the day. Darkness and light to you are both alike.

"For you yourself created my inmost parts. You knit me together in my mother's womb. I will thank you because I am marvelously made. Your works are wonderful and I know it well. My body was not hidden from you while I was being made in secret and woven in the depths of the earth. Your eyes beheld my limbs, yet unfinished in the womb. All of them were written in your book. They were fashioned day by day when as yet there was none of them.

"How deep I find your thoughts, Holy One. How great is the sum of them. If I were to count them, they would be more in number than the sand. To count them all, my life span would need to be like yours."

Love Mantra for Letting Go

I bless you
I release you

I set you free
I set me free

I let you be
I let me be

Good-bye Means God Be with You

Last words heard
clenched in the muscles,
held against grief
worked in the bone;
life pulls away
from the grey-eyed child.

Last words spoken
still harm, now
worked down
in remaining gaps
in the body, through
follicles, each Goodbye
of a lifetime pressed
in a strand
for the grey-haired child.

Grey is a passage
through which life can flow.
"God-be-with-you"
"God-be-with-you"
Hold on.
"God-be-with-you"
"God-be-with-you"
Let go.

After Dismembering

Not fixed perfection but
again-and-again completion,
unfolding, open-circling.

To re-member your Self
is to for-get
to get (Be)fore pain
to what you are
deeper down.

To re-member your Self
is to for-give,
to give (Be)fore to yourself
blessing: healing from
the wound by means of the wound
itself; and
comfort: deep strength with
deep peace.

Bless you, Be comforted.
From the moment
that holds you,
begin anew.

Loving the Body

I have lost my place.
My body has become
a foreign country.
I no longer know
its maps or rules.

What language it speaks
are silent to me or
frighten me to silence
by their strangeness.

They seem harsh.
They come from nerve,
and grate.

Even muscle groans
under their sounds.
Skin erupts in the effort
of trying to understand.

I am dried out
from loss of tears.
And sometimes
there are screams.

I grow suddenly dizzy,
caught in the white-out
of an inner tundra storm.
Without focus I cannot tell
if I am going somewhere
or holding still.

I want to move freely
in this country and
live here again.
I want to respond well
to its voices and weathers,
learn its new laws.
I want to feel its welcome again.
I want to be unafraid and peaceful
and know that, after all,
I was born here.

I need an interpreter in my own skin.
Friend, help me to find and keep place
    here.
Be doctor or lover.
Hold me, and remind me how.

Two Houses

This is my grieving house.
Like the Moon Houses of my mothers.
I withdraw here into open space filled
with comfortable red light to be apart.

It is like crawling inside an egg.
It is like being a seed aware
of itself rotting in the ground
but not understanding the strange new
shoots sprouting from its sagging wounds.

When I am inside my grieving house
I paint myself red for protection.
I practice parthenogenesis:
I give birth to myself.

The long deep love labor
of a screaming belly,
a belly in the brain,
a belly in the soul,
permitting my body
to be broken
among earth's grave
bones.

I swim in inner sea water
though I do not know how to swim.

Come near only if you are willing
to dye your skin with your own blood
and lie with me face down on the ground.

Later, we shall move out
to join the feast
in our common house of healing.

Scars

Grieving is an art
like surgery or verse,
essentially the art of healing
loss or losses unaccounted for.

Losses cut the soul
in twos and threes
a wide green gash
like the wound of
a tree cut down
suddenly.

So much more time
than expected
so slowly heals
the severed pieces
of the self shock-shattered
by guilt and rage
and the simple loneliness
of something missing,
the hug, the casual telephone talk,
the good occasional fight lost forever
to the harsh nonphysical world of death.

Grief lived faithfully heals itself
in time not fully.
Where once an open wound burned
    unbearably
now a thin transparent scar.

Still I know that till
the hour of my own death
the scar glows
and now and then bad weather
will come and waken the same old ache.
A scar is a now and then throb
that dies only with one's own death.

Dance for Me When I Die

A woman ran through a tunnel toward the ocean
  and she danced, she danced in the ocean.
A woman ran through a tunnel toward her death
  and they danced, they danced for her death.

> Nobody's grandmother
> I'll be a fairy
> godmother if you
> choose me
>
> How I'd love to be
> around with roses
> when you ring forth
> in glory
>
> So make a promise
> wish for wish—
> I'll sing to all
> your rainbow living
>
> If you will laugh
> once, weep a little,
> and dance for me
> when I die.

Daughter-rite

I sang at my mother's deathbed
and stood to honor the dream
of her life, pure and complete
(her name means Essence),
to honor the gift of the dream
passed on to me,
to receive the daughter-right,
her name;
then held my breath
and courted her death
with a vision of dancers,
a great invisible orchestra,
and pink roses;
courted my mother's death
and gave back breath
and became midwife
for her birthday into Paradise.

Awakening

The mother bird beats
against the bathroom window
for days—disrupting my sleep—
three hours each morning, her body
a battering ram into the larger world
she confuses for my house, against
whose glass wall she last saw
her child alive.

She cannot save him
from more life,
either way.

I, too, throw my body against
the Crystal Door.
It is not my intent to kill myself,
but to follow the lover/mate
who preceded me into the realms
of light we call paradise.

What I learn from this
is that I am awakening.

It is again time
of the morning star,
and I return with spring
to the ancient sea nest,
place where the trees
were born.

Now I can hear the call
back to the body
of those who love me,
and yield myself
to their hands.

We are not ready to go.
We are not yet happy
and well enough for heaven.

But together we can learn
to love and laugh with power
enough to walk safely
even on fire.

From *Midwives*

4.
From the depths of your long awaiting
from deprivation of the common
    from the milk of your devotion
    from the oceans of your care

                    Life will go on.

From the breast of the living God
                    Life will be borne.

About the Author

The Rev. Alla Renée Bozarth, Ph.D., was one of the first eleven women who were ordained as priests in the Episcopal church. The ordination of this group, which created a stir in ecclesiastical circles and drew international attention, took place in Philadelphia in 1974.

As a priest and also as a therapist, Dr. Bozarth practices "spiritual midwifery," guiding others to find emotional and spiritual health at Wisdom House in Sandy, Oregon.

Alla speaks and writes about the grief journey from personal experience, as one who has lost both of her parents and her husband. Her husband, also an Episcopal priest, died suddenly in 1985 at the age of thirty-seven.

Other Inspirational Works by Dr. Alla Bozarth

Audiotape: *Life Is Goodbye, Life Is Hello*
Gentle, Specific Help to Move through the Most Difficult
Stages of Grief

The original audio recording from which this booklet was
taken offers the added impact of hearing Alla in person.
This tape will provide comfort and help at times when
reading is too difficult or just not possible.

It's a particularly valuable resource for the troublesome
times when you're alone, or in the middle of the night when
sleep won't come.

> "Her message comes across with absolute
> clarity....Her approach is one of healing."
> *Publishers Weekly*

Running time: 60 minutes   ISBN: 0-89638-190-0 $9.95